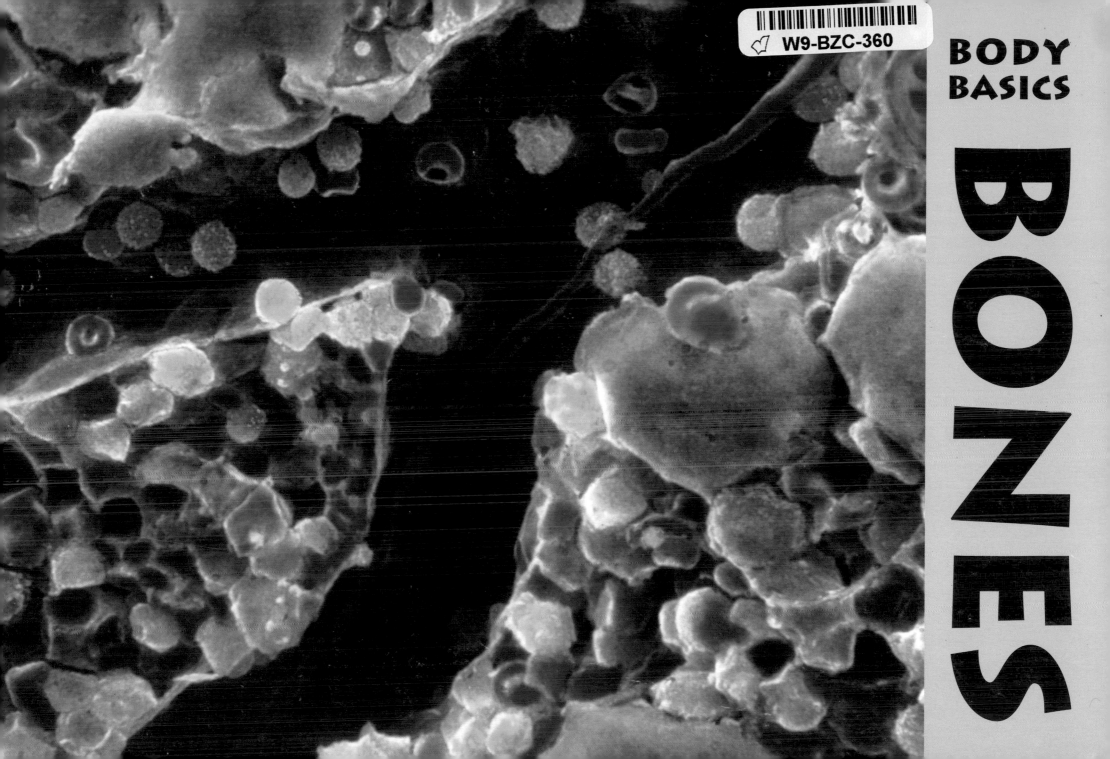

BODY
BASICS

BONES

Author: Anita Ganeri

Senior designer: Miranda Kennedy

Editor: Elise See Tai

Published by Tangerine Press, an imprint of
Scholastic Inc., 557 Broadway; New York, NY 10012

tangerine
Press
an imprint of
SCHOLASTIC
www.scholastic.com

Scholastic Australia Pty. Ltd; Gosford NSW
Scholastic New Zealand Ltd.; Greenmount, Auckland
Scholastic Canada Ltd.; Markham, Ontario
Scholastic UK; Coventry, Warwickshire

Created by Pinwheel
A Division of Alligator Books Ltd
Gadd House, Arcadia Avenue, London N3 2JU, UK

10 9 8 7 6 5 4 3 2 1

ISBN-10: 0-545-12045-4
ISBN-13: 978-0-545-12045-6

Printed in Malaysia

CONTENTS

Arms
The bones in your arms and fingers allow a wide range of movement.

Ribs
Your ribs protect your heart and lungs and allow you to breathe.

Pelvis
Your pelvis has a rounded shape for walking upright.

Legs
The leg bones are long and strong to carry your body's weight.

SKELETON

The bones in your body link together to make your skeleton. Your skeleton gives your body its shape and stops it from collapsing. Some bones protect your delicate organs and provide firm anchorage for your muscles so you can move.

SKELETON FACTS!

- YOUR SKELETON IS MADE UP OF 206 BONES.
- A NEWBORN BABY HAS 300 BONES, BUT SOME BONES *FUSE* TOGETHER AS THE BABY GETS OLDER.
- YOUR SKELETON MAKES UP ABOUT 15 PERCENT OF YOUR BODY WEIGHT.
- YOUR BACKBONE, RIBS, AND SKULL FORM YOUR *AXIAL* SKELETON.

BONES

Bones are living parts of the body, made up of bone tissue, blood vessels, and nerves. They are hard on the outside for strength, but soft and spongy inside for lightness. Despite their incredible strength, bones can sometimes break, but they can also heal themselves.

Finger bone
The finger bones are called *phalanges* (fuh-lan-jeez) (singular: *phalanx* (fal-angks).

Spongy bone
Spongy bone is made up of a mesh of pieces of bone with large spaces in between. This makes it lightweight so that your skeleton is not too heavy to move.

Finger nail
The nail is made
from hard, dead cells.
It grows from a part
of the skin called the
nail root.

**CROSS SECTION
OF A FINGER**

Fat layer
In the fingertip, a thick
layer of fat protects
the bone, blood
vessels, and nerves.

BONE FACTS!

- BONE IS SIX TIMES STRONGER THAN THE
  SAME WEIGHT OF STEEL.
- SOME BONES CONTAIN JELLYLIKE MARROW,
  WHICH MAKES RED BLOOD CELLS.
- THE SMALLEST BONES ARE THE *OSSICLES*
  (OS-I-KUH LZ) (EAR BONES), WHICH ARE
  THE ANVIL, HAMMER, AND STIRRUP INSIDE
  YOUR EARS.
- A BONE IS COVERED IN A THIN, TOUGH
  SKIN CALLED THE *PERIOSTEUM* (PER-EE-
  OS-TEE-UH M).

5

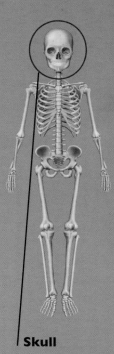

Skull

SKULL

Your skull is a jigsaw of more than 20 different bones. Fine, wiggly lines show where the bones are joined together. Some of these skull bones form a hard case to protect your delicate brain. Other bones hold your eyes in place and give your face its shape.

Eye socket
The eye sockets are bony hollows in the skull that hold your eyes in place and protect them.

SKULL FACTS!

- A BABY'S SKULL IS VERY SOFT, SO IT CAN CHANGE SHAPE AS IT IS BEING BORN.
- THE BONES IN YOUR FACE ARE ARRANGED IN PAIRS TO MAKE YOUR FACE LOOK SYMMETRICAL.
- YOUR SKULL HAS A HOLE FOR YOUR NOSE BECAUSE YOUR NOSE IS MADE FROM *CARTILAGE*, NOT BONE.
- PADS OF FAT, NERVES, AND BLOOD VESSELS CUSHION YOUR EYES IN YOUR EYE SOCKETS.

Cranium
The cranium is made of eight bones. It surrounds and protects your brain like a helmet.

Frontal bone
The frontal bone gives your forehead its round, bulging shape.

FRONT VIEW OF SKULL

Jaw joint
The jaw joint is the only movable joint in the skull. It allows your mouth to open and close.

Upper jaw
The upper jawbone is called the maxilla (mak-sil-uh). It is made up of several bones fused together.

Teeth
An adult has 32 teeth—16 in each jaw. Teeth are not bones. They are covered in enamel, the hardest material in the body.

Lower jaw
The lower jawbone is called the mandible (man-duh-buh l). It is U-shaped and stretches from ear to ear.

8

JAWS AND TEETH

The jaw is the lower part of your skull. The upper and lower jaw bones hold your teeth in place and allow you to eat. Your lower jaw moves up and down and from side to side so that you can chew your food. It is connected to the upper jaw by two joints on either side.

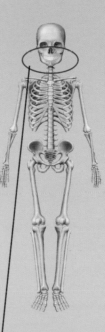

Jaws and teeth

JAW FACTS!

- The mandible (lower jawbone) is the only bone in the skull that moves.
- The mandible is the largest and strongest bone in the face.
- A young child has smaller jaws than an adult and only 20 baby teeth.
- Strong muscles along the sides of your face are important for chewing.

9

BACKBONE

The backbone (spine) is a long chain of bones that runs down the middle of your back. It is made up of 33 separate ringlike bones, called vertebrae (vur-tuh-bray) (singular: vertebra (vur-tuh-bruh). Your backbone is strong and flexible. It holds your body up and allows you to twist and bend. Your spinal cord, a delicate bundle of nerves, runs through the middle of the vertebrae.

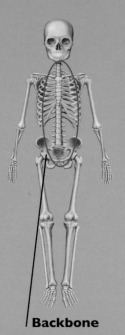

Backbone

BACKBONE FACTS!

- Your spine is S-shaped to balance your body and lessen the shock when you walk or run.
- The atlas vertebra is named after the Greek god, Atlas. In legend, he carried the weight of the world on his shoulders.
- Each vertebra can move a little, but put together, they make your spine flexible enough to bend over.
- There are cushionlike pads of cartilage between the vertebrae for absorbing shock when walking or running, for example.

Sacrum (sak-ruh m)
The sacrum is a large bone between the last lumbar vertebra and the coccyx.

SPINE

Atlas and axis
The top two vertebrae
support your skull and
allow you to nod and
shake your head.

**Cervical
vertebrae**

Thoracic vertebrae
Your 12 pairs of ribs are
attached to your 12 thoracic
(chest) vertebrae.

Lumbar vertebrae
The five lumbar vertebrae
in your lower back carry the
weight of your upper body.

Coccyx
The four lowest vertebrae
are fused together to
form the coccyx (kok-siks)
(tail bone).

RIB CAGE

Your ribs are attached to your spine. They curve to the back to form a strong, bony cage around your chest. They help protect your heart and lungs. The top seven pairs of ribs connect to your *sternum* (stur-nuh m) (breastbone) at the front of your chest.

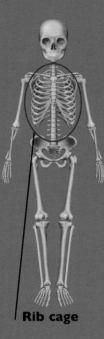

Rib cage

RIB CAGE FACTS!

- RIBS ARE THIN AND SPRINGY SO THAT THEY CAN ABSORB KNOCKS WITHOUT BREAKING.
- MOST PEOPLE HAVE 12 PAIRS OF RIBS. VERY FEW PEOPLE HAVE 11 OR 13 PAIRS.
- YOUR RIB CAGE MOVES UP AND DOWN SO THAT YOU CAN BREATHE IN AND OUT.
- A BROKEN RIB IS DANGEROUS BECAUSE IT CAN PUNCTURE YOUR LUNGS OR HEART.
- THERE ARE STRONG MUSCLES AND TOUGH LIGAMENTS IN BETWEEN YOUR RIBS.
- ALL RIBS ATTACH TO THE SPINE.

Clavicle (klav-i-kuh l)
The clavicles (collar bones) sit above the first ribs. They help support the weight of your arms.

Sternum
The sternum is a flat, platelike bone in the middle of the chest.

True ribs
The top seven pairs of ribs connect to your sternum by thin strips of cartilage.

False ribs
The next three pairs of ribs down are joined at the front to the lowest true ribs.

Floating ribs
The lowest two pairs of ribs are only attached to your spine.

RIB CAGE

ARMS AND HANDS

The bones in your arms and hands are designed to perform an amazing number of tasks. They allow you to carry out a wide range of highly complex movements, from throwing a ball into the air to writing with a pen, or picking up a tiny pin.

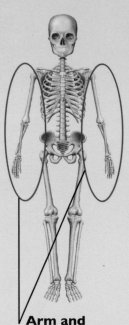

Arm and hand bones

Scapula (skap-yuh-luh)
The *scapula* (shoulder blade) is a large, flat bone held in place by your shoulder muscles and ligaments.

Humerus (hyoo-mer-uh s)
The *humerus* is a long bone in the upper arm.

Radius (rey-dee-uh s)
The *radius* is one of two long bones in the lower arm.

Ulna (uhl-nuh)
The *ulna* is one of the long bones in the lower arm.

ARM FACTS!

- THE UPPER AND LOWER ARM BONES ARE CONNECTED AT YOUR ELBOW JOINT.
- YOUR SHOULDER IS AN INCREDIBLY FLEXIBLE *BALL-AND-SOCKET* JOINT. (SEE P. 20.)
- THE BONES IN YOUR ARMS AND SHOULDERS HAVE ROUGH SURFACES WHERE MUSCLES ARE ATTACHED.
- YOUR *FUNNY BONE* IS ACTUALLY A NERVE THAT RUNS OVER THE END OF THE ULNA.

HAND FACTS!

- HALF OF THE BONES IN YOUR BODY ARE FOUND IN YOUR HANDS AND FEET.
- THERE ARE 27 BONES IN EACH OF YOUR HANDS.
- YOUR KNUCKLES ARE THE ENDS OF YOUR *METACARPALS* (MET-UH-KAHR-PUH LZ).
- YOUR WRISTS ARE MADE OF EIGHT SMALL BONES CALLED *CARPALS* (KAHR-PUH LZ).

Phalanges
The phalanges are the bones in your fingers. Hingelike joints allow your fingers to bend.

COLORED X-RAY OF HAND

Metacarpals
The metacarpals are the five long bones in your hands that make up your palms.

Thumb
The thumb contains only two bones, whereas the other phalanges (fingers) all have three bones.

Carpals

PELVIS AND HIPS

Your pelvis is a bowl-shaped ring of bones that supports the weight of your upper body and protects the organs in your lower body. The two main bones in your pelvis are called the *coxal* (kok-suh l) bones (hip bones). Each is made up of three smaller bones that are fused together. These are the *ilium* (il-ee-uh m), *ischium* (is-kee-uh m), and *pubic* (pyoo-bik) bones.

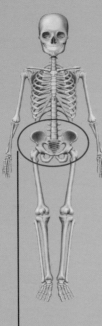

Pelvis and hips

Hip socket
The ball-shaped top of the thighbone fits into the hip socket. This joint is like the shoulder. It allows for a wide range of movements.

PELVIS FACTS!

- A woman's pelvis is wider than a man's.
- Your pelvis is connected to your spine at the *sacrum*, a bone made of five fused vertebrae. (See pp. 10–11.)
- A human pelvis is rounded to balance our bodies over our feet as we walk.
- Large muscles are attached to the *ilia* (il-ee-uh) to bend and straighten your legs.

16

X-RAY OF PELVIS

Ilium (plural: ilia)
The ilium is the bone you can feel when you press your hand on your hip.

Pubic bone
The two pubic bones meet at the front of the pelvis. They are joined by a strip of cartilage.

Ischium (plural: ischia)
The ischia in your buttocks are the bones that take your weight when you sit down.

HIP FACTS!

- Your hip joints are where your legs connect to your pelvis.
- The hip joint is a type of ball-and-socket joint. The top of the thighbone moves in the hip socket.
- Both the ball and socket are lined with cartilage to allow smooth movement.
- The deep hip socket in your pelvis is called the *acetabulum* (as-i-tab-yuh-luh m).
- If a hip joint gets damaged, it can be replaced with an artificial joint made from metal, plastic, or ceramic.

LEGS AND FEET

Your legs and feet are built for moving and standing upright. The bones in your legs are thick and strong to carry your body's weight. Your feet are long and wide for balance, and have springy arches for pushing your legs off the ground. Each leg is made up of four bones—the *femur* (fee-mer) (thighbone), *tibia* (tib-ee-uh) (shin bone), *fibula* (fib-yuh-luh) (calf bone), and *patella* (puh-tel-uh) (kneecap). There are 26 bones in each of your feet.

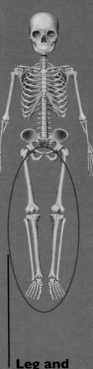

Leg and foot bones

FEET FACTS!

- THE 26 BONES IN EACH FOOT ARE ARRANGED IN A SIMILAR WAY TO THE BONES IN YOUR HANDS.
- TWO BONES IN YOUR FEET CARRY MOST OF YOUR WEIGHT—THE *CALCANEUS* (KAL-KEY-NEE-UH S) AND *TALUS* (TEY-LUH S).
- THE BONES KNOWN AS YOUR ANKLE ARE ACTUALLY THE ENDS OF THE TIBIA AND FIBULA.
- YOUR FOOT BONES FORM THREE STRONG ARCH SHAPES; TWO ALONG YOUR FOOT AND ONE ACROSS.
- A SYSTEM OF LIGAMENTS, TENDONS, AND MUSCLES HOLDS YOUR FOOT BONES TOGETHER.

LEG FACTS!

- THE FEMUR (THIGHBONE) IS THE LONGEST AND STRONGEST BONE IN YOUR BODY.
- THE TOP OF THE FEMUR FITS INTO THE HIP SOCKET. THE BOTTOM SITS IN TWO SHALLOW DIPS IN THE TIBIA.
- THE PATELLA (KNEECAP) IS A SMALL BONE THAT PROTECTS THE KNEE JOINT.
- YOUR KNEES ARE HINGELIKE JOINTS THAT ALLOW YOU TO BEND YOUR LEGS. (SEE P. 20.)

Metatarsals (met-uh-tahr-suh lz)
The metatarsals are the five long bones just before your toes start.

Phalanges
The phalanges are the short bones in your toes that balance your body.

Big toe
Your big toes have only two bones, while each of the other toes has three.

Tibia
The tibia (shin bone) is a long, strong bone in the lower leg.

Fibula
The fibula (calf bone) is also long, but thinner than the tibia.

LEG BONES

Patella
(kneecap)

Fibula
(calf bone)

Tibia
(shin bone)

Calcaneus
The calcaneus is the heel bone. It sticks out behind the foot.

Tarsals
Part of the ankle is made up of seven bones called *tarsals* (tahr-suh lz). They are strong, but not very flexible.

LEGS AND FEET

X-RAY OF SKELETON

Neck
The pivot joint in your neck allows you to turn your head from side to side.

Shoulder
In a ball-and-socket joint, the ball-shaped end of one bone fits into the cup-shaped socket of another.

Elbow
Your elbow is a hinge joint. It opens and closes like the hinge of a door.

Ankle
Some of the bones in your ankle move by sliding against each other. This is where the surfaces of two flat bones are held together by ligaments.

Joints

Joints are places where two bones meet. They allow your body to bend, turn, and twist. There are about 100 joints all over your body—in your knees, ankles, shoulders, neck, back, and even deep inside your ears. Joints are divided into different types, depending on how the bones move. In most joints, the bones are held together by strong straps, called ligaments, that allow them to move without bending too far.

Hip
The ball-and-socket joint in your hip allows you to move your hip in a circular motion.

Knee
The hinge joint in your knee allows you to bend and straighten your leg.

Toes
You also have tiny hinge joints in your toes and fingers.

KNEE JOINT

Femur (thighbone)
The femur meets the tibia at the knee joint.

JOINT FACTS!

- THE KNEE JOINTS ARE THE LARGEST JOINTS IN YOUR BODY.
- THE SMALLEST JOINTS ARE BETWEEN THE TINY BONES DEEP INSIDE YOUR EARS.
- SOME JOINTS, LIKE THOSE IN YOUR SKULL, ARE FIXED AND DO NOT ALLOW ANY MOVEMENT.
- WHEN A JOINT IS DISLOCATED, THE BONES ARE NO LONGER IN LINE.
- IF YOU ARE "DOUBLE-JOINTED," IT MEANS THAT YOU HAVE EXTRA-LONG LIGAMENTS IN YOUR JOINTS AND SO CAN BEND THEM FARTHER THAN NORMAL.

Patella

Fibula

Ligaments
Ligaments are strong straps of tissue that connect bone to bone.

Synovial fluid
Synovial (si-noh-vee-uhl) fluid in the joint keeps the joint "oiled." The synovial membrane produces the synovial fluid.

Tibia

Cartilage
Pads of cartilage cover the ends of the bones to allow easy movement and prevent wear and tear.

MOVING BONES

Bones form the framework of your body and joints allow your bones to move. But the power to move your whole body comes from your muscles. Many muscles are attached to your bones by strong bands, called *tendons* (ten-duh ns). When you move, your brain sends signals to your muscles, telling them to contract (pull) on your bones.

Hamstrings (ham-strings)
The *hamstring* muscles in the back of your thigh bends your knee and hip.

Achilles (uh-kil-eez) tendon
The *Achilles* tendon attaches the gastrocnemius to the heel.

Gastrocnemius (gas-trok-nee-mee-uh s)
The *gastrocnemius* muscle bends your knee and straightens your ankle.

Soleus (soh-lee-uh s)
The *soleus* muscle allows your foot to point downward.

Sartorius (sahr-tohr-ee-uhs s)
The *sartorius* muscle turns your leg and bends it at the hip.

MOVING BONE FACTS!

- MUSCLES CAN ONLY PULL, NOT PUSH, SO THEY OFTEN WORK IN PAIRS. THE HAMSTRINGS AND QUADRICEPS WORK TOGETHER TO BEND AND STRAIGHTEN YOUR LEGS.
- THE LARGEST MUSCLE IS THE GLUTEUS MAXIMUS IN YOUR BOTTOM AND UPPER THIGHS.
- THE SARTORIUS IS THE LONGEST MUSCLE. IT RUNS FROM YOUR PELVIS ACROSS YOUR THIGH TO YOUR KNEE.
- THE SMALLEST MUSCLE IS THE STAPEDIUS MUSCLE. THERE IS ONE IN EACH EAR. THEY ATTACH TO THE TINY BONES INSIDE YOUR EARS.
- MORE THAN 600 MUSCLES IN YOUR BODY HELP MOVE YOUR BONES.

Triceps (try-seps)
Your *triceps* muscle straightens your arm.

Deltoid (del-toid)
The *deltoid* muscle moves your shoulder to raise your arm.

CLOSE-UP OF A HUMAN BODY RUNNING

Biceps (by-seps)
Your *biceps* muscle bends your elbow.

Gluteus maximus (gloo-tee-uhs mak-suh muh s)
The gluteus maximus muscle straightens your thigh at the hip.

Quadriceps (kwod-ruh-seps)
The muscle in the front of your thigh straightens your leg. It is made up of four different muscles.

HUMAN SKELETON

The hundreds of bones that make up your skeleton all have scientific names, as well as common ones. You can see some of them below. This makes it easier for doctors and scientists to make sure they are talking about the same bones. For example, the femur is your thighbone; the clavicle is your collar bone; and the vertebrae are your backbones.

DID YOU KNOW?

OUR SKELETON FOLLOWS THE SAME BASIC DESIGN FOUND IN THOUSANDS OF SPECIES OF MAMMALS. THE BODY IS SUPPORTED MAINLY BY THE SPINE WITH A SKULL, RIB CAGE, AND FOUR LIMBS. THE HUMAN SKELETON HAS ONE BIG DIFFERENCE. IT HOLDS OUR BODIES UPRIGHT SO WE CAN WALK ON TWO LEGS.

THE HAND

Carpals
The carpals make up most of your wrist.

Metacarpals
The metacarpals are long bones in the palms of your hands.

Phalanges
The phalanges are the finger bones.

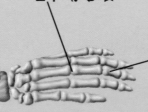

Cranium
The cranium is the main part of the skull.

Maxilla

Mandible

Eye socket

Clavicle
A clavicle is a collar bone. There is one

Rib
The 12 pairs of ribs form the rib cage.

Ulna
The ulna is the inner bone in the forearm.

Radius
The radius is the outer bone in the forearm.

Femur
The femur is the thighbone.

Tibia
The tibia is the shin bone in the lower leg.

Humerus
The humerus is the long bone in the upper arm.

Spine
The spine (backbone) is made up of vertebrae.

Pelvis
The pelvis is a bowl-shaped ring of bones.

Patella
The patella is the kneecap.

Fibula
The fibula is the calf bone in the lower leg.

25

Coccyx
The coccyx (tail bone) is made from four vertebrae joined together.

Sacrum
The sacrum is part of your pelvis and is made of five vertebrae joined together.

28

HUMAN SKELETON REAR VIEW

This rear view of a human skeleton shows the bones of your spine (backbone) clearly. It runs down the center of your body and supports your head, arms, and legs. From this angle, your spine looks completely straight but from the side, it has a slight S-shape. This helps to balance your body.

Atlas
The top vertebra in your spine.

Axis
The second vertebra in your spine.

Cervical vertebrae
The seven vertebrae in your neck.

Thoracic vertebrae
The 12 vertebrae in your chest.

Lumbar vertebrae
The five vertebrae in your lower back.

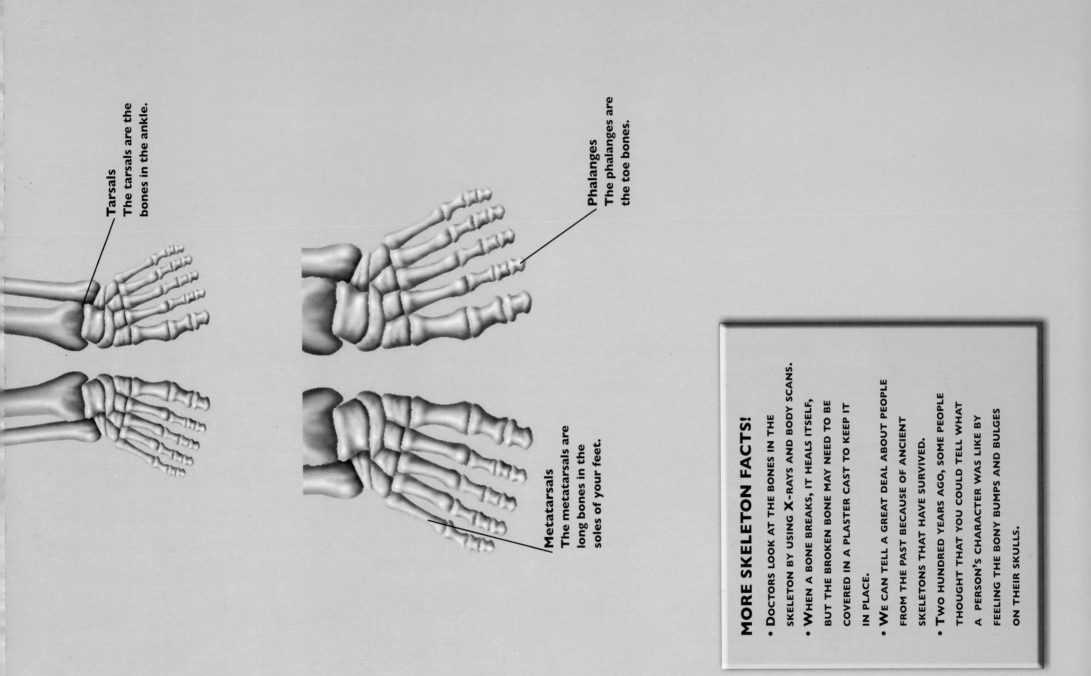

Tarsals
The tarsals are the bones in the ankle.

Phalanges
The phalanges are the toe bones.

Metatarsals
The metatarsals are long bones in the soles of your feet.

MORE SKELETON FACTS!

- DOCTORS LOOK AT THE BONES IN THE SKELETON BY USING X-RAYS AND BODY SCANS.

- WHEN A BONE BREAKS, IT HEALS ITSELF, BUT THE BROKEN BONE MAY NEED TO BE COVERED IN A PLASTER CAST TO KEEP IT IN PLACE.

- WE CAN TELL A GREAT DEAL ABOUT PEOPLE FROM THE PAST BECAUSE OF ANCIENT SKELETONS THAT HAVE SURVIVED.

- TWO HUNDRED YEARS AGO, SOME PEOPLE THOUGHT THAT YOU COULD TELL WHAT A PERSON'S CHARACTER WAS LIKE BY FEELING THE BONY BUMPS AND BULGES ON THEIR SKULLS.

Glossary

AXIAL

Refers to something that runs from top to bottom along a line.

BALL-AND-SOCKET JOINT

A joint where the ball-shaped top of one bone fits into the cup-shaped socket of another.

BLOOD VESSELS

The tubes that carry blood around your body.

CARTILAGE

A smooth, gristly substance that forms the end of your nose and cushions the bones in a joint.

DISLOCATED

When the bones in a joint are forced out of place by a knock or a fall.

ENAMEL

An extremely hard material that covers the outside of your teeth.

FUSE

Join together

HINGE JOINT

A joint that opens and closes like the hinge of a door.

LIGAMENT

Band of tough, fiberlike material that holds the bones together in a joint.

MARROW

A jellylike substance found inside some large bones that makes new red and white blood cells.

ORGAN

A particular body part, such as your heart, lungs, and liver.

PHALANGES (SINGULAR: PHALANX)

The bones of the fingers and toes.

PIVOT JOINT

A joint where the end of one bone rotates in a round space of another.

SKELETON

The framework of bones inside your body.

SYMMETRICAL

Something that is the same on either side of a middle point.

TENDON

Tough cord that connects a muscle to a bone.

TISSUE

Groups of cells that work together to form your skin, muscle, blood, and so on.

Index

Picture Credits

Illustrations by Kuo Kang Chen with the exception of those listed below.

Cover (background): PROF. P. MOTTA / DEPT. OF ANATOMY / UNIVERSITY "LA SAPIENZA", ROME / SCIENCE PHOTO LIBRARY; 1: ROBERT BECKER / CUSTOM MEDICAL STOCK PHOTO / SCIENCE PHOTO LIBRARY; 2–3: ROGER HARRIS / SCIENCE PHOTO LIBRARY; 4: PROF. P. MOTTA / DEPT. OF ANATOMY / UNIVERSITY "LA SAPIENZA", ROME / SCIENCE PHOTO LIBRARY; 4–5: ANATOMICAL TRAVELOGUE / SCIENCE PHOTO LIBRARY; 7: PAUL RAPSON / SCIENCE PHOTO LIBRARY; 8–9: FRIEDRICH SAURER / SCIENCE PHOTO LIBRARY; 10–11: PASIEKA / SCIENCE PHOTO LIBRARY; 12–13: FRIEDRICH SAURER / SCIENCE PHOTO LIBRARY; 14: PASIEKA / SCIENCE PHOTO LIBRARY; 15: SCIENCE PHOTO LIBRARY; 16–17: SCIENCE PHOTO LIBRARY; 18–19: ANTOINE ROSSET / SCIENCE PHOTO LIBRARY; 20: GUSTOIMAGES / SCIENCE PHOTO LIBRARY; 21 (left): SCIENCE PHOTO LIBRARY; 21 (right): CNRI / SCIENCE PHOTO LIBRARY; 22: ROGER HARRIS / SCIENCE PHOTO LIBRARY; 23: ROGER HARRIS / SCIENCE PHOTO LIBRARY; 27–28: ROGER HARRIS / SCIENCE PHOTO LIBRARY.